ideals® EASTER

*Heaven and earth
and saints and friends
and flowers are
keeping Easter Day!*
—AUTHOR UNKNOWN

ideals

NASHVILLE, TENNESSEE

Daffodils

Edna Jaques

I shall remember daffodils
and cool sweet grasses blowing,
the high white cliffs a-shining
and wind upon the sea.
I shall remember daffodils
against a sunny window,
yellow as new sweet butter
in an old brown wooden churn;
a golden cup to drink the wine
of any April morning;
and love just waiting to be met
at every winding turn.
I shall remember daffodils
in the hazy mist of sunrise
like candles through a frosted glass
upon a winter night,
or tiny floating bells of gold
too frail for any ringing.
I shall remember daffodils
to hold for my delight.

The Breath of God

Myra Brooks Welch

The breath of God
stirs to life the green
and growing things
that sleep beneath the sod.
He breathes on me,
and in each resurrected flower,
the living Christ I see.

Earth's Resurrection

Edith Shaw Butler

Winter's long, long sleep is over.
Brooks have burst their icy chains.
Fields and hills each day grow greener,
coaxed by warming sun and rains.

Birdsong fills the waking woodlands.
Swelling bud foretells the flower.
Hearts in joyous acclamation
greet the resurrection hour.

Before You Thought of Spring

Emily Dickinson

Before you thought
    of spring,
except as a surmise,
you see, God bless
    his suddenness,
a fellow in the skies
of independent hues,
a little weather-worn,
inspiriting habiliments
of indigo and brown.

With specimens of song,
as if for you to choose,
discretion in the interval,
with gay delays he goes
to some superior tree
without a single leaf,
and shouts for joy
    to nobody
but his seraphic self!

Photograph © Judy Kennamer/Shutterstock

Spring Awakening

Phyllis C. Michael

I heard the purple crocus sing,
"Wake up, you sleepyhead!
Come on, get up, you tulips, now,
get up! Get out of bed!"

I watched the tulips slowly rise
and stretch their leafy arms;

I knew that soon, yes, very soon,
the world would share their charms.

In Easter dress they too would call,
"Wake up! Wake up! It's spring!"
I knew, for faith woke in my heart—
I heard the crocus sing.

Flower Chorus

Ralph Waldo Emerson

Oh, such a commotion under the ground,
when March called, "Ho, there! Ho!"
Such spreading of rootlets far and wide,
such whisperings to and fro!
"Are you ready?" the Snowdrop asked.
" 'Tis time to start, you know."
"Almost, my dear!" the Scilla replied.
"I'll follow as soon as you go."
Then "Ha! Ha! Ha!" a chorus came
of laughter sweet and low,
from millions of flowers under the ground—
yes, millions beginning to grow.

"I'll promise my blossoms," the Crocus said,
"when I hear the blackbird sing."
And straight thereafter, Narcissus cried,
"My silver and gold I'll bring."
"And ere they are dulled," another spoke,
"the Hyacinth bells shall ring."

But the Violet only murmured, "I'm here,"
and sweet grew the air of spring.

O the pretty brave things,
    thro' the coldest days
imprisoned in walls of brown,
they never lost heart
    tho' the blast shrieked loud,
and the sleet and the hail came down;
but patiently each wrought
    her wonderful dress,
or fashioned her beautiful crown,
and now they are coming
    to lighten the world
still shadowed by winter's frown.
And well may they cheerily laugh "Ha! Ha!"
in laughter sweet and low,
the millions of flowers under the ground,
yes, millions beginning to grow.

Woodland Springtime

Mabel Fundingsland

The trees have donned their
   spring gowns
in varied shades of green.
Pussy willows are bursting forth
from every twig, it seems.

The little brook is rushing on
o'er pebbles white and clean,
and woodland folk are scamp'ring
as if waking from a dream.

Cloven tracks of dainty fawn
are traced in soft, warm earth,
and song birds sing a welcome
as they join in spring's rebirth.

A wondrous note of harmony
with happiness to share;
it's springtime in the woodland
and God is everywhere.

A Simple Spring Birthday

Anne Kennedy Brady

Soon after returning from Easter break in my senior year of college, I took a job as a clown. I figured I should put my imminent theater degree to work while I waited for Hollywood to call, and spring felt like a great time to try something new, so I contacted a friend of a friend who ran a children's entertainment company. After a week studying face painting and the finer points of balloon animals, I was entrusted with a costume and sent on my first gig: a birthday party.

I expected some version of the simple parties I grew up with, so I was alarmed when I pulled up to a five-star event. The birthday boy lived in an affluent neighborhood close to downtown Seattle, and his beautiful home sat on an expansive manicured lawn which was currently housing a bouncy castle, a catered buffet, and forty squealing first-graders. Parents mingled and sipped drinks in the backyard. I hiked up the front walk in my baggy pants and loud suspenders and rang the doorbell.

For the next three hours, I painted faces and sculpted balloon animals in the April sunshine, thinking about the birthday parties of my youth. There had been no bouncy houses or outside entertainment, and our guest list was capped at seven or eight friends. But my brothers and I *lived* for those parties. We'd spend weeks agonizing over whom to invite and deciding on a party theme. My birthday

always fell near Easter, so one year I asked for a "bunny party." Mom bought an ice cream cake shaped like a log, nestled it in green Easter grass, and created ears and a face out of wafer cookies and licorice. The table centerpiece featured small stuffed rabbits, one of which each girl gleefully took home at the end of the party. Another year, I requested a "flower party." Mom and Betty Crocker conjured up a lemon bundt cake and filled the center with daffodils and tulips. My friends skipped home after the festivities, ribbon streamers fluttering from their handmade floral crowns.

In addition to those parties with friends, I always looked forward to our family birthday parties. Every year on our actual birthday, we were allowed to choose the menu for dinner, after which we'd have a small celebration with just the five of us. Before dessert and presents, we strapped on pointed paper hats and passed around silly favors Mom had found at the dollar store. We played whatever game we could think up with the favors— a parachute-man accuracy test from the top of the stairs, a toy-car race across the kitchen floor, or a paper-airplane distance contest. I can barely remember the presents I got during those family parties, but every time I see a fifty-cent cardboard glider kit at the drugstore, I remember the year Dad got stuck with the hot-pink plane that wouldn't fly.

A few years ago, my parents flew out to visit my husband and me in Chicago over Easter. It was one of those years my birthday and the holiday fell on the same day, and we decided to celebrate in true Kennedy fashion. That evening, Dad strung up a paper banner we'd rescued from the clearance bin at Target while Mom whipped up a taco casserole—my perennial birthday dinner choice. After the meal, we competed for "Best Easter-Themed Sculpture" using modeling clay from a nearby discount shop. One of my new favorite memories is of my forty-year-old husband insisting that his amorphous blob of clay was, in fact, an archangel. We all became kids again for the bargain price of a dollar-store trinket.

At the end of my stint as a clown at that gala birthday party on the epic lawn, the hostess handed me a twenty-dollar tip and a hefty slice of birthday cake. I thanked her and complimented her on the party. She grinned, pleased. "We just want our boy to have the perfect birthday, you know?" I smiled back and nodded. I did know. I just wish I could have told her that all she really needed were a few cardboard glider kits—and maybe some taco casserole.

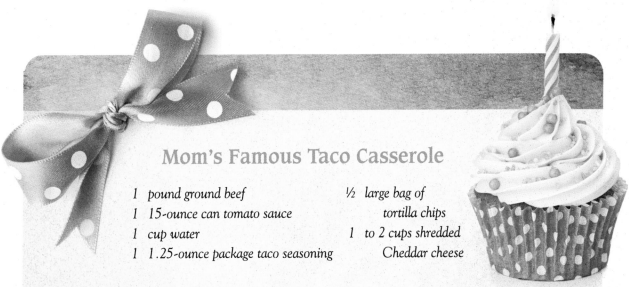

Mom's Famous Taco Casserole

1 pound ground beef
1 15-ounce can tomato sauce
1 cup water
1 1.25-ounce package taco seasoning

½ large bag of
     tortilla chips
1 to 2 cups shredded
     Cheddar cheese

Preheat oven to 350°F. In a large, oven-safe skillet over medium-high heat, brown ground beef. Remove from heat and strain off excess fat. Return meat to the stove, lower heat, and add tomato sauce, water, and taco seasoning, stirring until well combined. Crush tortilla chips lightly in your hands and add to mixture in skillet; the pieces can be fairly large. Stir mixture until all chips are wet. Sprinkle cheese evenly over top. Put skillet in oven and bake about 20 minutes, until cheese is bubbling and toasty. Remove and let cool for at least 10 minutes. Makes 6 to 8 servings.

Bits & Pieces

To plant a garden is
to believe in tomorrow.
—*Audrey Hepburn*

The day the Lord created
hope was probably the same
day He created Spring.
—*Bern Williams*

The glory of the spring, how sweet!
The newborn life, how glad!
What joy, the happy earth to greet
in new, bright raiment clad!
Divine Redeemer, Thee I bless;
I greet Thy going forth;
I love Thee in the loveliness
of Thy renewèd earth.
—*Thomas Hornblower Gill*

In the spring, at the end of the
day, you should smell like dirt.
—*Margaret Atwood*

It is always springtime
in the heart that loves God.
—*Saint John Vianney*

Some old-fashioned things like fresh
air and sunshine are hard to beat.
—*Laura Ingalls Wilder*

Where flowers bloom, so does hope.
—*Lady Bird Johnson*

Earth, with her thousand
voices, praises God.
—*Samuel Taylor Coleridge*

My favorite weather is
bird-chirping weather.
—*Terri Guillemets*

Springtime is the
land awakening.
The March winds are
the morning yawn.
—*Lewis Grizzard*

Through My Window

Spring into Shape

Pamela Kennedy

In spring, when tree branches begin to plump up with new leaves and garden plots fill with buds and blossoms, my mailbox seems to sprout catalogs. Since they always feature what's in style for the coming season, along about March they're filled with summer wear and models prancing gracefully on sunlit beaches or basking on the decks of sailboats. And although I don't personally plan on doing much prancing or basking, they do serve to remind me that I'll soon have to shed my layered look for something cooler and, perchance, a bit more revealing than my jeans and tunic-length sweaters. Such thoughts inevitably lead me to consider "getting into shape."

Last spring I mentioned this to my daughter, who has no need to consider such things since she is thirty-five years younger than I am and is busy *staying* in shape. She is a helpful daughter, however, and in her gentle and loving way, she suggested some ideas.

First, she downloaded an app to my smartphone that allows me to track everything I eat. This miraculous app totals my calories all day long and lets me know when I have reached my daily goal . . . usually around noon. She also suggested engaging the services of a personal trainer at the gym where my husband and I are members.

"You already go several times a week," my daughter said. "I'm sure they have trainers. And there might be some springtime discounts!"

True, I have been working out there for a couple of years, but I like my routine: thirty minutes on the elliptical machine watching the morning news, then thirty minutes of exercises on various machines and a floor mat while chatting with a friend. Although not super vigorous, it's at least a routine that allows me to break a sweat and assuage my guilt. But my daughter has a point. The trainers must be there for a reason.

Her last suggestion was to "find a kind of exercise you love," but I can tell you right now that is not going to happen. I do, however, want my adult daughter to know that I value her opinion, so I checked out a few options.

One crisp morning, I tagged along with a friend to a Pilates class, which, I was quickly disappointed to discover, had nothing to do with actual lattes. The class opened with some gentle stretches set to soothing music. I liked that. I could get used to that. But then the music kicked up a bit, and we started to do things that I truly believe are impossible. The instructor, an extremely calm and encouraging young woman, told us to lie on our mats and pull our navels into our backbones, then "scoop" our abdomens while stretching our arms forward and lifting our legs off the mat. She kept reminding us to breathe deeply, which was good because I was starting to see little sparkly objects and getting lightheaded from holding my breath. I'm not sure I ever saw my toes come up off the mat, and I can't even tell you where in the world my navel was in relationship to my spine. We did this kind of thing for about forty-five minutes. I learned a lot. In particular, I learned that Pilates and I were not in love.

So I signed up with a personal trainer. She was neither extremely calm nor encouraging, nor young, for that matter. She was, however, a very energetic and muscular fifty-something from Eastern Europe who may or may not still be fighting the Cold War.

"You need discipline, and you need to *vork hart!*" she announced when we first met. She jabbed her index finger toward the elliptical machine: "I see you on that machine. You go nowhere!" I was about to point out that it was bolted to the floor, but she was already heading toward the weights. For the next hour she put me through my paces and demonstrated challenging exercises with painful-sounding names like "plank" and "burpee" and "crunch." The "dead bug" sounded a bit more doable, but trust me, it wasn't. I think I was more in the market for exercises with names like "napping tiger," "rocking granny," and "meditating jellyfish." After my first (and last) hour with Brunhilda, even my hair hurt!

Photograph © by Cheryl Images/Shutterstock

When summer rolled around, I wasn't in much better shape than I had been in March. Fortunately, I didn't have much time to feel discouraged, because in late July the fall catalogs started showing up in my mailbox. And I am happy to report that they were filled with a lovely selection of stylish jeans and figure-flattering tunic tops. Maybe I'll start shaping up *next* spring.

Rain's Song

Patricia B. Dye

The rains that fall in April
sing a soft and gentle song.
It's a lullaby from nature
that says spring has come along.

There's a rhythm filled with promises
that hum with every breeze.
It's whistled by the willows
as the wind blows through their leaves.

The lyrics tell of tulips
and of others soon to bloom.
The notes create a symphony
of color from God's plume.

The melody is in the air,
so come and sing along.
Enjoy the rains of April
and the beauty of their song.

April's Song

Gertrude Dicks

An April day is never still,
with growing sounds on every hill,
and here the song of spring is heard
in joyful singing of each bird.

The tapping of a gentle rain
plays notes upon my windowpane,
and tulips sleeping in their bed
awake to drumbeats overhead!

The breezes sigh, as breezes do,
when once again the skies are blue,
and look for newly budding leaves
to entertain with melodies.

The season always seems to start
when I hear music in my heart,
and April's tune is sure to say
that spring, at last, is here to stay!

Photograph © sarsmis/Shutterstock

Easter Hiding and Hunting

Catherine Otten

*I*n our little neighborhood, the corner store served to officially announce the arrival of all holidays. With the beginning of Lent came fresh smoked fish, kegs of herring, even more types of cheese than usual, and Mama's special herring rollmops, all prominently displayed to make the obligatory meatless meals easier to bear. But the candy window, heralding Easter, was always the star display. Soft, yellow, sugary chicks lay in neat rows between solid milk-chocolate rabbits, elegant in their foil wrappers. Tall glass jars of jellybeans decorated the back shelves of the candy corner, while tiny tin frying pans of candy sunny-side-up eggs joined other Easter novelties priced at a penny each on the top shelves of the glass candy case.

Most neighborhood children abstained from candy during Lent, and we were no exception. Still, every so often a sweet might fall into our hands during those six weeks of penance, and we never turned down an offered treat. So before Ash Wednesday, each one of us secured a shoebox to hide our treasures until Easter.

"What's all this?" demanded Mama one day as she cleaned the shelves in my closet.

"It's my Lent candy," I explained, grabbing my precious box off of the trash heap.

"Throw it out," Mama ordered mercilessly. "We'll have bugs all over the place. The closet is no place for food!"

We should have known better than to try to hide anything in those days before Easter. Mama always scrubbed and cleaned the house thoroughly to make ready for Resurrection Day. Nothing and nowhere was safe from the broom, the scrub brush, and Mama's eagle eyes—especially the one she claimed to have in the back of her head.

"Throw this one out too," said Mama, tossing my little sister's Lent box on the heap. "You kids can't eat that stale old stuff anyway."

My sister and I carried our boxes of goodies to the basement that day. We carefully selected new hiding places for our sweet savings and prayed Mama's cleaning wouldn't venture there. Just a few more days until Easter, and then we could finally enjoy the fruits of our sacrifices!

Finally Easter arrived. Our Easter always started with the earliest church service of the morning, singing with the sunrise. "Alleluia, alleluia! Let the loud hosannas ring!" Those loud hosannas were thrilling, even at five o'clock on a very cold morning. The glorious music announced what our hearts knew—"Christ is risen!"

The mile-long trek home from church was full of anticipation of the Easter basket hunt that would start the moment we got home. I will never forget the year our big shaggy shepherd dog found our baskets first; he must have begun his hunt as soon as we left for church that morning. But the disappointment over our ruined sweets was overcome by our amusement at the tableau the poor dog made, lying guilty and quiet in the middle of all those destroyed Easter nests, sick, well, as a dog!

After the hunt, we stealthily retrieved our candy boxes from their hiding places while Mama was busy frying bacon and scrambling eggs. There was no sweeter taste in the world than that hard, stale loot, so anticipated for so long!

But we made sure to save room, because we knew breakfast was going to be a meal to remember. Mama had spent Holy Saturday preparing mountains of delicious baked goods, and the meal was made even more special by the cousins, aunts, and uncles who had gathered at our house after church. Taking our places around the big table, we bowed our heads while Papa said grace. And as bright Easter sunlight streamed through the windows, we listened to Papa ask God's blessing. We were so grateful for all that we had been given that year—the candy bounty and less tangible gifts—and for our loved ones around us.

Easter and Spring

Lansing Christman

*E*ach year, spring arrives almost hand in hand with Easter, offering an appropriate ritual for the observance of the Resurrection. As we rejoice in the new season of birth, hope, and faith, we remember the great joy the risen Christ brought to His people on the day He conquered death and rose from the grave.

Each season has its role to play, and spring assumes the great responsibility of restoring cheer and strength. It emerges from winter's cold darkness with songs and flutes, buds and blossoms, bringing renewed hope and the solace of faith.

That first spring blossom is glorious to the eye, as the meaning of the Resurrection is glorious to the heart and soul of man. We cannot ignore the greatness of all things in nature, with their aching beauty and dramatic annual rebirth. Neither can we ignore that behind nature's great changes—behind all life itself—is the work, labor, and love of the Master of all.

It is impossible to close our eyes to the beauty unfolding around us each spring: the new green, the flowers, the longer days of sun, the warming land, and the budding trees and plants. Even if we could, we would not be able to shut out the birdsongs resounding from orchard and woodland, from dooryard to pasture, from field and fen.

In the same way, we cannot close our eyes and ears to the glorious message of Easter, expressed in hymns and from pulpits across the land. Through sweeping music and passionate words, each person becomes aware that he is made for something far greater than the accumulation of wealth and material things. He understands that the only riches of value come in the form of faith, love, and following the Spirit. With such truth before him, he finds there is no longer room in his heart for greed and hate. Instead, there is room only for love and compassion— room only for peace and the richness of its content.

Photograph © Juliette Wade/Gap Photos, Inc.

Easter Morning

Ruth H. Underhill

What a lovely Easter morning—
smiles on every face;
children waiting eagerly
to start the annual race.

Colored eggs are hidden well,
and chocolate bunnies too;
see the cheery colors—
purple, orange, blue.

A chick of yellow marshmallow
peeks from beneath a stump;
a tiny chocolate rabbit
peers around a grassy clump.

Lovely woven baskets all
await sweet sugary fill,
as the blazing sun comes up
o'er the emerald, grassy hill.

Photograph © Ufuk ZIVANA/Shutterstock

An Easter Story

Michelle Grigsby

Everyone I know associates Easter with eggs, and I'm no different. As I watch my chickens each spring, I rejoice in the humble egg's promise of new life—a perfect illustration of the season's message.

One year, as Easter approached, I was looking forward to teaching the lesson of the egg in my Sunday school class. But when I asked the children where eggs come from, their answer surprised me.

"Bunnies!" all twelve students shouted.

My confusion must have been obvious, because one girl rushed to explain: "It's on TV. A white rabbit lays chocolate eggs."

I realized what they meant. I'd seen the commercial, but it didn't have much to do with the lesson I wanted to teach. I wondered how I could help them understand.

The following Sunday, before leaving for church, I checked on my chicken coop. One hen, Henney Penney, puffed her feathers to twice her size when my rooster, Rudy, got close. She was guarding a dozen eggs.

That's when it hit me: How many of the kids had ever seen a real egg hatch? Watching an ordinary, beige egg turn into a live, peeping chick—with bright BB-pellet eyes, downy feathers, and tiny feet—was like watching a miracle. That would be an Easter message they'd never forget!

As I hunted for a box to hold the eggs, I tried to ignore a nagging doubt. *Should I really bring a chicken to church?* I thought of a certain church lady—a good Christian with very strong opinions—who had objected to my son's flashy Bible cover.

"It's a New Testament," I'd assured her as she eyed the brightly colored jacket.

"Well," she'd sniffed, "it looks like a Betty Crocker cookbook!"

I had a vision of my little bantam hen pooping on the ecclesiastical carpet, leading to a prim reprimand that chickens don't belong in church. But then I remembered Jesus' words in Matthew 23:37: "How often I have longed to gather your children together, as a hen gathers her chicks under her wings" (NIV).

"That settles it," I told Henney Penney. I poked holes in the lid of a straw-filled cardboard box and transferred Penney and her eggs into it.

The box was waiting on the table when the children arrived for class. They eyed it curiously, and when they'd taken their seats I lifted the lid. The children gasped. Penney blinked in the sudden light and ruffled her feathers, but soon settled and clucked contentedly.

"What do you think Penney's brought with her?" I asked. I lifted her up to reveal twelve eggs—one for each child! "I'll bring Penney back next week and you can see your eggs turn into baby chicks on Easter." The children giggled and agreed, excited.

As I went to bed the next Saturday night, the doubt returned. It took twenty-one days for a bantam hen egg to hatch. What if I'd miscounted? What if Penny's temperature wasn't just right? I switched off the light and prayed, *Please let at least one egg hatch for them.*

The church parking lot was packed the next morning. Everyone always came for Easter service, but why did the Sunday school wing have a crowd? I wove my way through with my cardboard box.

"Is that Penney?" a woman asked me.

"Did the eggs hatch yet?" a man said.

My heart pounded. The entire congregation and every single Sunday school class had come to see Penney and her eggs! Even the pastor was there.

"It's a perfect sermon illustration!" he said. "Would you bring her into the church?"

I nodded and followed him to the sanctuary as a pack of children cheered and plunked themselves on the stage at the front. *Okay, God,* I thought, lifting the lid. *Time for an Easter miracle!*

A gasp went up. There was Penney with not one, but six wobbly chicks! Three were already dry and fluffy as dandelion down, and three were still wet from their shells. The last six eggs had cracked enough to reveal new chicks just emerging.

Photograph © Friedrich Strauss/Gap Photos, Inc.

I looked up, beaming, from Penney's new family—right into the face of the parishioner I'd dreaded. She was gazing at the chicks, as happy and amazed as the little girl in front of her who asked, "How did you get the eggs to hatch right on Easter?"

"God decides when the eggs hatch," I said. "He knew this was the perfect time!"

And the perfect place—in His own house, where all new life begins.

I Believe He Heard

Roy Zylstra

Secluded in a grove of birch,
I came upon this small white church.
Its bell to me tolled soft and clear,
"He is risen; He is here."

Inside, the pews were old and worn,
the altar cloth was patched where torn;
through stained-glass windows very near,
the sun was filtered amber clear.

In the place a choir would stand
stood the youngsters hand in hand.
The youngest seemed no more than four;
their number I would judge a score.

Raising eyes to Him above
in simple, true, unquestioned love,
just as though we were not there,
together they began their prayer.

"Lord, please hear us as we pray
on this joyous Easter Day.
Guide our feet along Your way
as we live from day to day.

"Teach us kindness, faith, and love,
look upon us from above.
Let our hearts be ever true,
dear Lord Jesus, unto You."

A tender closeness filled the air;
I felt somehow that He was there
among us in the church that day
because He heard the children pray.

Outside, the bell tolled soft and clear,
"He is risen; He is here."

APRIL MORNING by Randy Van Beek.
Image © Randy Van Beek/Art Licensing

Busy Hands at Easter

Pamela Love

Hands are often busy
at this special time of year,
dyeing eggs and gardening
as Easter Day draws near;

dressing up and baking,
and helping others too.
Yes, when it is this time in spring,
hands have so much to do.

But their most important task
is when they're held quite still,
when we thank God that
　　through Jesus,
His promise was fulfilled.

Photograph © Friedrich Strauss/Gap Photos, Inc.

Communion

Margaret Rorke

Oh, Lord, we are a hungry crowd,
so needing to be fed.
Pass unto us, with spirits bowed,
Thy flesh-embodied bread.
Our lips are parched. We hold our cup
for blessing most divine.
Pass unto us and let us sip
Thy purple-blooded wine.

Oh, take us to the upper room,
where once so long ago,
amid Your own encircling gloom,
You helped the twelve to know
that You would be a part of them
who'd take the bread You broke,
and go from old Jerusalem
to spread the word You spoke.

Oh, Lord, behold our sacrament—
the table we've prepared,
on which the food our Father sent,
the grain and grape is shared.
In spirit break our bread today
and touch the chalice too,
for us who use this means to say
that we remember You.

Sleeping Christians

Edna Moore Schultz

The disciples were so weary
in the dark Gethsemane,
and their eyelids grew sleep-heavy
(they relaxed contentedly).
Soon they were sleeping, O so calmly,
while the precious Lamb of God
agonized in yonder garden
sweating anguished drops of blood!
Could they not have watched
    and waited
for one silent solemn hour
when the enemy attacked
with such vicious cruel power?
His disciples still are weary,
sleeping when they ought to pray.
May they stir themselves to service
on this blessed Easter Day.

Song

Charles G. Blanden

What trees were in Gethsemane,
what flowers there to scent,
when Christ for you and Christ for me
into His garden went?

The fragrant cedar tree was there,
the lily pale and slim;
they saw His grief, they heard
    His prayer,
and wept their dews for Him.

And that is why the cedars green
and why the lilies white
do whisper of the Master's love
in gardens, late at night.

Photograph © Clive Nichols/Gap Photos, Inc.

THE VOICE OF HIM that crieth in the wilderness, Prepare ye the way of the LORD, make straight in the desert a highway for our God. Every valley shall be exalted, and every mountain and hill shall be made low: and the crooked shall be made straight, and the rough places plain: And the glory of the LORD shall be revealed, and all flesh shall see it together: for the mouth of the LORD hath spoken it.

—Isaiah 40:3–5

AND THEY BROUGHT the colt to Jesus, and cast their garments on him; and he sat upon him. And many spread their garments in the way: and others cut down branches off the trees, and strawed them in the way. And they that went before, and they that followed, cried, saying, Hosanna; Blessed is he that cometh in the name of the Lord: Blessed be the kingdom of our father David, that cometh in the name of the Lord: Hosanna in the highest. And Jesus entered into Jerusalem, and into the temple: and when he had looked round about upon all things, and now the eventide was come, he went out unto Bethany with the twelve.

—Mark 11:7–11

NOW WHEN JESUS was in Bethany, in the house of Simon the leper, There came unto him a woman having an alabaster box of very precious ointment, and poured it on his head, as he sat at meat. But when his disciples saw it, they had indignation, saying, To what purpose is this waste? For this ointment might have been sold for much, and given to the poor. When Jesus understood it, he said unto them, Why trouble ye the woman? for she hath wrought a good work upon me. For ye have the poor always with you; but me ye have not always. For in that she hath poured this ointment on my body, she did it for my burial. Verily I say unto you, Wheresoever this gospel shall be preached in the whole world, there shall also this, that this woman hath done, be told for a memorial of her.

—Matthew 26:6–13

And I said unto them, If ye think good, give me my price; and if not, forbear. So they weighed for my price thirty pieces of silver. And the LORD said unto me, Cast it unto the potter: a goodly price that I was prised at of them. And I took the thirty pieces of silver, and cast them to the potter in the house of the LORD. —Zechariah 11:12–13

Then one of the twelve, called Judas Iscariot, went unto the chief priests, And said unto them, What will ye give me, and I will deliver him unto you? And they covenanted with him for thirty pieces of silver. . . . Then Judas, which had betrayed him, when he saw that he was condemned, repented himself, and brought again the thirty pieces of silver to the chief priests and elders, Saying, I have sinned in that I have betrayed the innocent blood. And they said, What is that to us? see thou to that. And he cast down the pieces of silver in the temple, and departed, and went and hanged himself. —Matthew 26:14–15; 27:3–5

For dogs have compassed me: the assembly of the wicked have inclosed me: they pierced my hands and my feet. I may tell all my bones: they look and stare upon me. . . . They gave me also gall for my meat; and in my thirst they gave me vinegar to drink. —Psalms 22:16–17; 69:21

And when they were come unto a place called Golgotha, that is to say, a place of a skull, They gave him vinegar to drink mingled with gall: and when he had tasted thereof, he would not drink. And they crucified him, and parted his garments, casting lots: that it might be fulfilled which was spoken by the prophet, They parted my garments among them, and upon my vesture did they cast lots. . . . Now from the sixth hour there was darkness over all the land unto the ninth hour. And about the ninth hour Jesus cried with a loud voice, saying, Eli, Eli, lama sabachthani? that is to say, My God, my God, why hast thou forsaken me? Some of them that stood there, when they heard that, said, This man calleth for Elias. And straightway one of them ran, and took a spunge, and filled it with vinegar, and put it on a reed, and gave him to drink. The rest said, Let be, let us see whether Elias will come to save him. Jesus, when he had cried again with a loud voice, yielded up the ghost. —Matthew 27:33–35; 45–50

DEATH SHALL NOT KEEP HIM

THEREFORE MY HEART is glad, and my glory rejoiceth: my flesh also shall rest in hope. For thou wilt not leave my soul in hell; neither wilt thou suffer thine Holy One to see corruption. Thou wilt shew me the path of life: in thy presence is fulness of joy; at thy right hand there are pleasures for evermore. . . . But God will redeem my soul from the power of the grave: for he shall receive me. Selah.

—Psalms 16:9–11; 49:15

· · · · · ·

IN THE END of the sabbath, as it began to dawn toward the first day of the week, came Mary Magdalene and the other Mary to see the sepulchre. And, behold, there was a great earthquake: for the angel of the Lord descended from heaven, and came and rolled back the stone from the door, and sat upon it. His countenance was like lightning, and his raiment white as snow: And for fear of him the keepers did shake, and became as dead men. And the angel answered and said unto the women, Fear not ye: for I know that ye seek Jesus, which was crucified. He is not here: for he is risen, as he said. Come, see the place where the Lord lay. And go quickly, and tell his disciples that he is risen from the dead; and, behold, he goeth before you into Galilee; there shall ye see him: lo, I have told you. And they departed quickly from the sepulchre with fear and great joy; and did run to bring his disciples word.

—Matthew 28:1–8

· · · · · ·

WHOM GOD HATH raised up, having loosed the pains of death: because it was not possible that he should be holden of it. . . . Because thou wilt not leave my soul in hell, neither wilt thou suffer thine Holy One to see corruption. . . . He seeing this before spake of the resurrection of Christ, that his soul was not left in hell, neither his flesh did see corruption.

—Acts 2:24, 27, 31

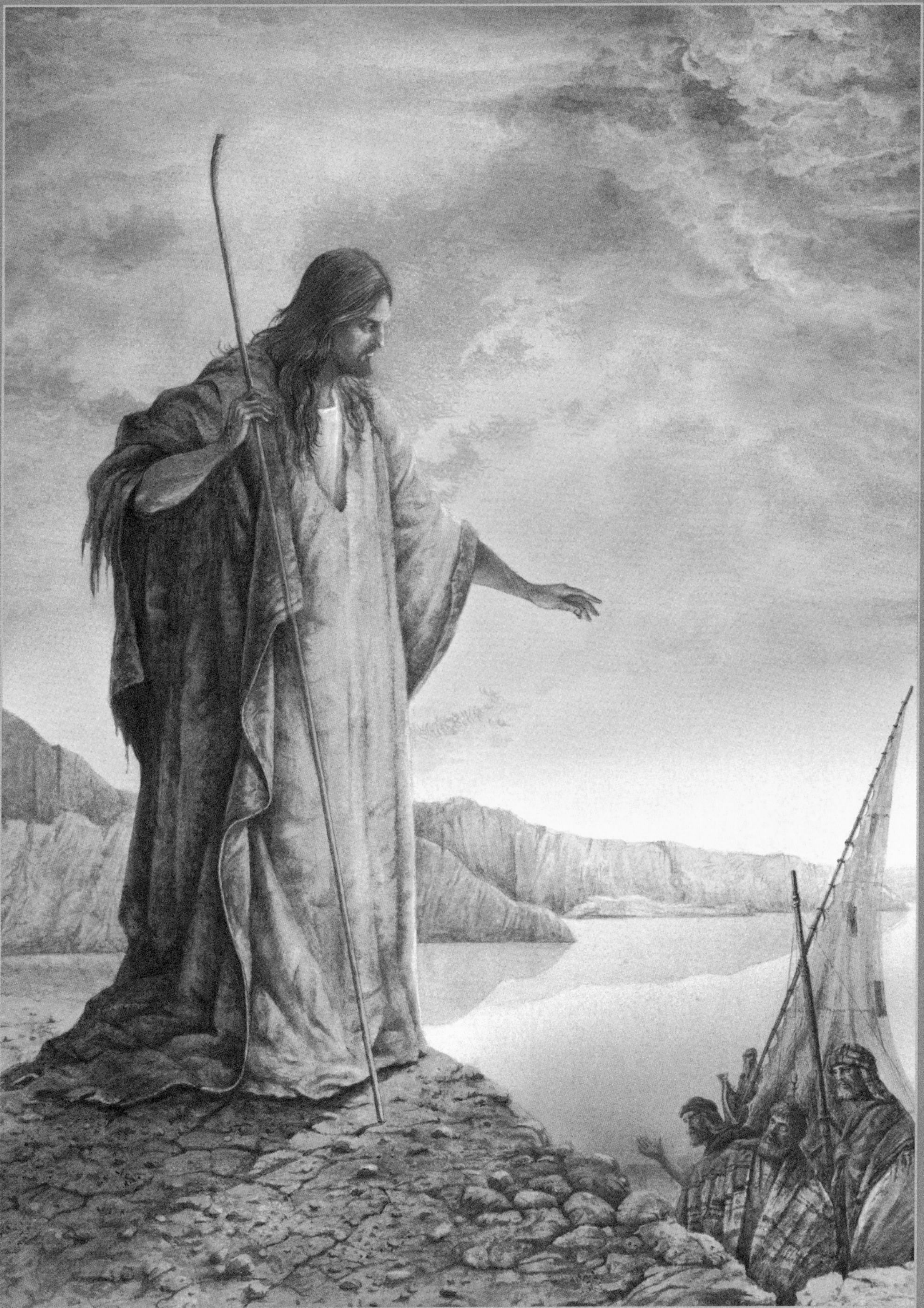

The Greatest Love Story

Doris B. Clearman

The greatest love story ever told
was written with blood, in drama, bold,
by a Heavenly Father who gave His Son
to bear the sins of everyone.

Mocked and reviled by greed's blind sight,
men turned to hate—forsook the right.
They placed on His head a thorn-plaited crown,
on His shoulders a cross, which weighted
    Him down,
and stumbling He struggled up Calvary's way.
Oh! What a tragic and terrible day!

As they suspended, between heaven and earth,
God's only Son—our King from birth,
all of our sins were heaped on Him.
As the day turned dark and the sun grew dim,
an earthquake shook the rocks and sod;
a soldier whispered, "The Son of God."
Then, agonizing on the tree,
Christ Jesus prayed for you and me,
"Father, forgive, they do not know
how much I care and love them so."
How could we be so blind and deaf,
disregarding all but self?
When Jesus died to save our souls,
greater love could not be told.

Yet the love story continues today,
in God's own tender, loving way.
He raised His Son from death's cold tomb
to bring us joy, dispel the gloom.
For the self-same Christ who was crucified
lives in our hearts—Christ is alive!

Easter

Clyde L. True

Behold! The stone was rolled away,
which gives us hope of endless day.
The tomb could not our Lord retain;
the bonds of death were all in vain.

All doubt and sorrow, death and gloom,
were left within the empty tomb,

and hope and gladness, life and light,
dispelled the darkness of that night.

For centuries the earth has moved
within the cycle and has proved
that life comes with returning spring,
and Christ to us new life doth bring.

The Resurrection

Jonathan Henderson Brooks

His friends went off and left Him dead
in Joseph's subterranean bed,
embalmed with myrrh and sweet aloes,
and wrapped in snow-white burial clothes.

Then shrewd men came and set a seal
upon His grave, lest thieves should steal
His lifeless form away and claim
for Him an undeserving fame.

"There is no use," the soldiers said,
"of standing sentries by the dead."
Wherefore they drew their cloaks around
themselves and fell upon the ground—
and slept like dead men, all night through,
in the pale moonlight and chilling dew.

A muffled whiff of sudden breath
ruffled the passive air of death.

He woke and raised Himself in bed,
recalled how He was crucified,
touched both hands' fingers to His head,
and lightly felt His fresh-healed side.

Then with a deep, triumphant sigh,
He coolly put His grave-clothes by:
folded the sweet, white winding sheet,
the toweling, the linen bands,
the napkin—all with careful hands—
and left the borrowed chamber neat.

His steps were like the breaking day:
so soft across the watch He stole,
He did not wake a single soul,
nor spill one dewdrop by the way.

Now Calvary was loveliness:
lilies that flowered thereupon
pulled off the white moon's pallid dress,
and put the morning's vesture on.

"Why seek the living among the dead?
He is not here," the angel said.

The early winds took up the words,
and bore them to the lilting birds,
the leafing trees, and everything
that breathed the living breath of spring.

He Is Risen

Pamela Perry Blaine

It was dark outside as we woke up and began getting ready for church. I was excited to get up early on Easter—I loved going to the sunrise service.

We attended church regularly for as long as I can remember, but Easter Sunday was different. There was something special about getting up before the sun. The air was extra crisp, and as the sky slowly lightened, the birds began chirping as if to announce the forthcoming sunrise.

We made our way down the gravel road to the church, located only a block from our house. I could hear the gravel crunching beneath my feet and tried to walk carefully so I wouldn't mark my new white shoes that I thought were almost too pretty to wear. I was especially excited to get to church this Sunday because my cousin Suzanne and I were singing a duet in the Easter program. We had rehearsed diligently and wanted to do our best.

More people than usual came to church on Easter Sunday. An atmosphere of expectancy filled the sanctuary as everyone was seated and the music began to play. Suzanne and I took our places in the front pew near the piano. The pastor spoke a few words of welcome, and the program began.

The choir sang "In the Garden," "The Old Rugged Cross," and "There Is a Fountain," with narration interspersed between songs. Then the moment came—the narrator read scripture that served as our cue: "'Father, into your hands I commit my spirit.' When he had said this, he breathed his last" (Luke 23:46 NIV). As soon as the scripture ended, Suzanne and I stood and began to sing the old spiritual, "Were You There When They Crucified My Lord?" Even as a child, I knew that in some mysterious way I had been there, and that the Lord had paid a debt He did not owe because I owed a debt I could not pay.

When our song ended, the narrator read the final scripture: "Now upon the first day of the week, very early in the morning, [the women] came unto the sepulchre, bringing the spices which they had prepared. . . . And, behold, there was a great earthquake: for the angel of the Lord descended from heaven, and came and rolled back the stone from the door, and sat upon it. His countenance was like lightning, and his raiment white as snow: And for fear of him the keepers did shake, and became as dead men. And the angel answered and said unto the women, Fear not ye: for I know that ye seek Jesus, which was crucified. He is not here: for he is risen, as he said" (Luke 24:1, Matthew 28:2–6).

At the very moment he finished, the choir broke into joyful singing, "Christ the Lord is risen today! Alleluia!" And as everyone filed out of the church toward home, I saw that the sun had risen as well and was streaming through the front door.

I ran down the gravel road toward home after that sunrise service. In my excitement, I forgot all about my new white shoes until I got home and saw them dusty and scuffed. I wondered if the women who found the empty tomb thought

about their shoes. Then I wondered what had become of the now unnecessary spices they had carried to the tomb. I decided the women had probably forgotten all about them; it's impossible to think about shoes or spices when you have just seen an earthquake, an empty tomb, and an angel saying, "He is risen!"

The service was over, but Easter continued that day when we returned home. I peeked into the kitchen and saw four coffee cups on the table awaiting our return. Each cup held a different colored liquid—red, green, yellow, and blue— and in a pan next to the coffee cups sat the eggs Mama had boiled the night before. I smiled. Part of the fun of Easter Day was coloring eggs. Mama made her own colors with water, vinegar, and food coloring, and we used a waxy crayon to write

names or designs on the eggs. There was no limit to the creations we could make! My brother and I colored Easter eggs and took turns hiding and finding them while Mama baked a cake and drew a picture of the cross and the empty tomb in the icing. She rarely had time for such things, but this was a special day. This was Easter Sunday, and its message rang in all of our hearts: "He is risen!"

This Easter I will again wake early to attend sunrise service. And as the sun rises in the sky and streams through the church doors, I will once more be reminded that "He is risen!" How awesome to know that the same God who created the sunrise loves us and wants to live in our hearts.

Sunrise Service

Pamela Love

Our eyes may look sleepy,
our clothes, not quite neat.
We may stifle a yawn.
We might shuffle our feet.

But music and Gospel
together combine
to waken our hearts
at this glorious time.

And though it's still early,
with minds now awake,
we give thanks to Jesus,
who died for our sake.

CHARMING TRANQUILITY II
by Nicky Boehme.
Image © Nicky Boehme/
Art Licensing

An Easter Gift

Diane Dean White

*T*he days were warm and the azaleas were in full bloom by mid-March. It had been a busy time for the children, adjusting to a new school and new friends after moving from Michigan to a suburb of Atlanta. The relative warmth and the spring flowers helped us appreciate our new home. We had joined a nearby church where we met several friendly people who included us in social events, always thinking of our children as well.

Still, as Easter approached, we missed our family back in the Midwest. At night, I shared my feelings with my husband about the area not quite feeling like home yet. I was concerned about the kids, and how different it was for them to be in a southern city. We both decided that the church family would be a big help, since the people in the congregation came from all over, and we trusted that the Lord would work things out in His own timing.

One afternoon, I received a phone call from a lady I had come to know at church—our children were the same ages and I felt instantly drawn to her. She had called to invite us over for Easter dinner! I was touched by this generous offer and delighted to have something for the children to look forward to, as well as some much-needed fellowship for Steve and me.

After Easter services, we followed our new friends back to their home. It was a large, welcoming house, and my eyes immediately fell on a bowl of colorful Jell-O squares that had been included in the elegant buffet for the kids. The table was adorned with colored eggs and flowers, and the children were seated together so conversation flowed easily. I marveled at how God brings people into our lives at just the right time, and gave thanks for their friendship.

The year progressed, and we were beginning to feel like the South was somewhat "home," when Steve came in one day with big news. His company wanted him to consider another position, but it would mean moving back to Michigan!

I saw my excitement mirrored in our children's faces.

"Home again?" said our oldest son. "I vote yes!" The others were in total agreement.

The following days were filled with packing boxes, and soon our departure date was upon us. On the day before the move, as I wondered how we would get everything done, our Easter-dinner friends showed up with some people from the church and pitched right in. The day was a blur of activity, but I remember thanking them for being such an encouragement to us during the months we had lived there. My friend simply said, "Just pass it on." She took credit for nothing, instead praising the Lord for everything. I was so grateful they were in our lives.

After returning to Michigan, I realized I had neglected to get their address, so I wrote a letter to the church to request it. I received the strangest reply. The church remembered us and wished us well, but they had no record of a family with our friends' last name. I called the church secretary the next day, but she had no idea whom I could be referring to. I described the names and ages of the children, where they lived, and what cars they drove. She said she was sorry she couldn't help.

That evening when Steve got home, I told him about the letter and the conversation. How ridiculous was this? They had attended services and other functions with us! I even tried contacting them by telephone, but the number was disconnected.

Steve and I looked at each other in wonder. We weren't going to question God on this one, but we certainly thanked Him in prayer. And although many years have passed since then,

Photograph © Julietphotography/Shutterstock

every time I make Jell-O squares for our grandchildren, I remember a special Easter long ago, when God gave us warm and caring friends that we will never forget.

Family · Recipes

Greek Yogurt Waldorf Salad

3 cups chopped apples	Zest of a medium lemon
1 cup chopped celery	2 teaspoons fresh lemon juice
½ cup chopped, toasted pecans, walnuts, or almonds	1 teaspoon granulated sugar
	1 teaspoon honey
¼ cup dried cherries or raisins	½ teaspoon ground cinnamon
¼ cup vanilla Greek yogurt	¼ teaspoon ground nutmeg

In a large bowl, combine apples, celery, nuts, and cherries; set aside. In a small bowl, mix yogurt with lemon zest, lemon juice, sugar, honey, cinnamon, and nutmeg. Pour dressing over the fruit mixture, and stir until coated. Refrigerate until ready to serve. Makes 6 to 8 servings.

Spicy Bacon Potato Salad

3 pounds red potatoes, peeled and cubed	1 tablespoon sriracha or chili sauce (extra to taste)
¼ teaspoon salt	3 to 4 slices cooked bacon, crumbled
2½ tablespoons white vinegar	¼ cup chopped green onion
¾ cup mayonnaise	Paprika, to taste
¼ cup sour cream	

In a large pot, cover potatoes with cold water, about 1 inch above the potatoes. Bring to a boil; reduce heat and simmer, stirring occasionally, until potatoes are fork-tender—about 8 minutes. Drain potatoes and move to a large mixing bowl. Add salt and vinegar and combine gently with a rubber spatula. Cool 15 minutes. In a small bowl, combine mayonnaise, sour cream, and sriracha or chili sauce; fold into cooled potatoes. Top with bacon, green onion, and paprika. Makes 6 to 8 servings.

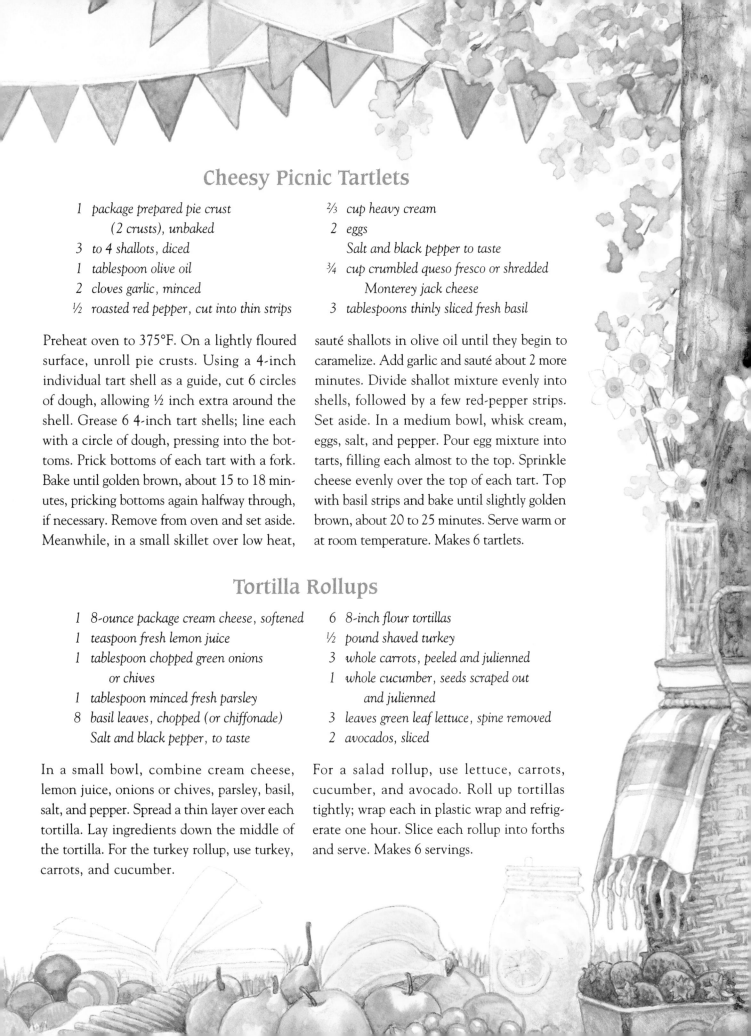

Cheesy Picnic Tartlets

1 package prepared pie crust
   (2 crusts), unbaked
3 to 4 shallots, diced
1 tablespoon olive oil
2 cloves garlic, minced
½ roasted red pepper, cut into thin strips

⅔ cup heavy cream
2 eggs
   Salt and black pepper to taste
¾ cup crumbled queso fresco or shredded
   Monterey jack cheese
3 tablespoons thinly sliced fresh basil

Preheat oven to 375°F. On a lightly floured surface, unroll pie crusts. Using a 4-inch individual tart shell as a guide, cut 6 circles of dough, allowing ½ inch extra around the shell. Grease 6 4-inch tart shells; line each with a circle of dough, pressing into the bottoms. Prick bottoms of each tart with a fork. Bake until golden brown, about 15 to 18 minutes, pricking bottoms again halfway through, if necessary. Remove from oven and set aside. Meanwhile, in a small skillet over low heat,

sauté shallots in olive oil until they begin to caramelize. Add garlic and sauté about 2 more minutes. Divide shallot mixture evenly into shells, followed by a few red-pepper strips. Set aside. In a medium bowl, whisk cream, eggs, salt, and pepper. Pour egg mixture into tarts, filling each almost to the top. Sprinkle cheese evenly over the top of each tart. Top with basil strips and bake until slightly golden brown, about 20 to 25 minutes. Serve warm or at room temperature. Makes 6 tartlets.

Tortilla Rollups

1 8-ounce package cream cheese, softened
1 teaspoon fresh lemon juice
1 tablespoon chopped green onions
   or chives
1 tablespoon minced fresh parsley
8 basil leaves, chopped (or chiffonade)
   Salt and black pepper, to taste

6 8-inch flour tortillas
½ pound shaved turkey
3 whole carrots, peeled and julienned
1 whole cucumber, seeds scraped out
   and julienned
3 leaves green leaf lettuce, spine removed
2 avocados, sliced

In a small bowl, combine cream cheese, lemon juice, onions or chives, parsley, basil, salt, and pepper. Spread a thin layer over each tortilla. Lay ingredients down the middle of the tortilla. For the turkey rollup, use turkey, carrots, and cucumber.

For a salad rollup, use lettuce, carrots, cucumber, and avocado. Roll up tortillas tightly; wrap each in plastic wrap and refrigerate one hour. Slice each rollup into forths and serve. Makes 6 servings.

The Dawn of Spring

Garnett Ann Schultz

There's magic in the dawn of spring;
we know it by the birds that sing,
the melting snow, the thawing creek,
the beauties nature-lovers seek,
perhaps a January thaw
with winter winds not quite as raw.

There's magic in the extra light;
the lengthened sunset bringing night,
expectancy in every heart,
soon tell that spring's about to start;
the catkins on the willow bough
remind us winter's over now.

The dawn of spring is everywhere—
within the forest, on the air,
as nature quickly comes alive,
no more a struggle to survive.
The buds and blossoms soon shall swell,
and naked trees in beauty dwell.

The sun now warms the earth below,
and tiny crocuses can grow.
The fields once brown begin to green,
and showers wash the whole world clean.
New hope and faith our God doth bring
because He sends the dawn of spring.

Photograph © kan_khampanya/Shutterstock

The Story of a Song

Christ Arose

Pamela Kennedy

Easter is a time of contrasts. We see the triumphal entry of Jesus into Jerusalem, as He is praised with waving palm branches and shouts of "Hosanna! Blessed is He who comes in the name of the Lord!" Then, only a week later, angry cries of "Crucify Him! Crucify Him!" ring through those same streets. There is the dark despair of death on a cross and burial in a borrowed tomb, followed by the blazing light of angels and the joyful announcement, "He is risen!" In "Christ Arose," Easter's stark contrast is captured in both words and melody by American preacher and hymn writer, Robert Wadsworth Lowry.

In the spring of 1874, while meditating on the angels' words to the women at Jesus' empty tomb (Luke 24:6–8), Lowry was inspired to pen "Christ Arose." The hymn's three verses contain a somber description of Christ in the grave, vainly sealed and guarded by Roman soldiers, sung to a dirge-like melody. But then each verse concludes with the up-tempo chorus, describing Christ's victory over death as He rose from the grave to shouts of "Hallelujah!" The author artfully blends words and melody to paint a powerful picture of the contrast between Christ's passion and victory.

Born in Philadelphia on March 12, 1826, Lowry graduated from the University of Lewisville (now Bucknell University), where he would return to teach English literature and later become the university's chancellor after a successful career as a Baptist pastor. Throughout those years he combined his proficiency in writing and theology with his interest in music to compose more than five hundred gospel songs and hymns. In 1868, after becoming the music editor at the Biglow & Main Publishing Company, Lowry collaborated with other gospel hymn writers, including Fanny Crosby and William Doane, to compose, compile, and edit a dozen Sunday school songbooks and hymn collections. Some of these contained additional hymns by Lowry, such as "Shall We Gather at the River?" and "Nothing But the Blood."

Lowry once said, "Music with me has been a side issue . . . I would rather preach a gospel sermon to an appreciative, receptive congregation than write a hymn." However, today it is for his hymns that Lowry is best remembered. And despite his assertion that he preferred the pulpit to the hymnal, it is through his legacy of hymns that Lowry continues to preach his most powerful sermons.

Christ Arose

Lyrics and melody by Robert Lowry (1826–1899)

1. Low in the grave He lay— Je-sus, my Sav-iour! Wait-ing the
2. Vain-ly they watch His bed— Je-sus, my Sav-iour! Vain-ly they
3. Death can-not keep his prey— Je-sus, my Sav-iour! He tore the

com-ing day— Je-sus, my Lord!
seal the dead— Je-sus, my Lord!
bars a-way— Je-sus, my Lord!

Up from the grave He a-rose,

He a-rose!

With a might-y tri-umph o'er His foes; He a-rose a

He a-rose!

Vic-tor from the dark do-main, And He lives for-ev-er with His saints to reign.

He a-rose! He a-rose! Hal-le-lu-jah! Christ a-rose!

He a-rose! He a-rose!

Life Unlimited

Esther York Burkholder

*I*t is an awesome thing to think that life could go on forever. And we who believe in the Christ of the first Easter know that it is true. Because He rose, we, too, can count on life unlimited. We are assured that beyond this swiftly passing time, there waits an eternity far better.

But Christ can also give us life unlimited here and now. When He enters into a human heart, horizons expand, capabilities multiply, life becomes more meaningful, and the influence we can have on others for good is infinite.

If any would have life unlimited, for now and for eternity, let him go to the One who created life in the beginning. He only waits to be asked.

Photograph © Natalia Klenova/Shutterstock

Thoughts at Easter

Beulah Sutton Waite

Be still, my lips, and hush your
　　aimless speaking
that I may listen; God is always seeking
to bring sweet peace into each life.
He'll gladly share our cares and strife.
Be still, my lips!

Beat softly, heart, that you may
　　hear God knocking;
have always near the key for your unlocking,
that His great love may enter in
to drive away all doubt and sin.
Beat softly, heart!

Think holy, mind, lest you should
　　find you're sinking
into the ways of vain and worldly thinking;
so strive to be a fertile field
where pure thoughts reap a bounteous yield.
Think holy, mind!

Rejoice, my soul, you've cause for
　　great elation:
God had a plan for all mankind's salvation.
He sent His Son to dwell on earth,
oh for our blessed Savior's birth—
rejoice, my soul!

Forevermore no greater love shall be:
upon the cross Christ's blood
　　was shed for me;
but death He conquered and arose,
His glorious victory to disclose—
oh joyful day!

Easter Joy

J. Harold Gwynne

Praise God from whom
   all blessings flow!
So say we when we pray;
we're thankful that our
   hearts can know
the joy of Easter Day!
'Tis joy of hope that lifts the soul
to ecstasy sublime,
that sees a distant, shining goal
beyond this realm of time!
And Easter stands for triumph true,
the greatest there can be;
for Christ has won this guerdon, too—

the joy of victory!
He conquered Satan's vast domain,
proved Victor in the strife,
that for His people He might gain
the joy and crown of life!
The joy of comfort Easter brings
for sorrows new and old;
we feel the Spirit's healing wings
around our lives enfold.
So give your hearts to fullest joy,
and be of one accord;
your songs of faith and love employ
to praise our risen Lord!

Everlasting Bloom

John B. Tabb

Like a meteor, large and bright,
fell a golden seed of light
on the field of Christmas night
when the Babe was born.

Then 'twas sepulchred in gloom,
till above His holy tomb
flashed its everlasting bloom—
flower of Easter morn!

Easter Prayer

Eileen Spinelli

Be blessed this day
by grassy hills,
by yellow blur
of daffodils,
by starling-song
and sky of blue,

by simple gifts,
by life made new,
by gentle stir
of hearts and trees—
be blessed, dear ones,
by all of these.

A Song for Easter

Rose Myra Phillips

Sing a song for Easter,
to the child and to the grown,
of One who loves so deeply
that He left His glory-throne
to be their risen Savior
and to bring to each a part

of the joyousness of heaven
to hold within his heart.

Ring the bells for Easter,
and let their glad notes flow
across the hills and valleys
for all the world to know.

CHERRY BLOOM HILLS *by Anthony Kleem.*
Image © Anthony Kleem/Art Licensing

Easter Message

Mamie Ozburn Odum

May this Easter message bring
all the beauty of the spring.
May every Easter wish come true
and beauty of the old renew.
May wonders of this Eastertide
fill hearts with hope, and peace, abide.
May Easter seasons grow more dear
with faith and trust throughout the year.
And may this coming Easter find
love in the heart of all mankind.

ISBN-13: 978-0-8249-1349-6

Published by Ideals
An imprint of Worthy Publishing Group
A division of Worthy Media, Inc.
Nashville, Tennessee

Printed and bound in the U.S.A.
Printed on Weyerhaeser Lynx. The paper used in this publication meets the minimum requirements of American National Standard for Information Sciences—Permanence of Paper for Printed Materials, ANSI Z39.48-1984.

Publisher, Peggy Schaefer
Editor, Melinda L. R. Rumbaugh
Copy Editors, Anne Kennedy Brady, Debra Wright
Designer, Marisa Jackson
Permissions and Research, Kristi West

Cover: Photograph © Roman Bilan/500px
Inside front cover: *Light Pink and Dark Tulips* by Joanne Porter. Image © Joanne Porter/Art Licensing
Inside back cover: *Early Spring Flowers* by Joanne Porter. Image © Joanne Porter/Art Licensing
Sheet Music for "Christ Arose" by Dick Torrans, Melode, Inc. Additional art credits: Pages 1, 10–11, 50–51, 54, and back cover art by Kathy Rusynyk. The following pages contain art © [the artist]/Shutterstock.com: 3, antipathique; 4–5, Iriskana; 6, wacomka; 8, vso; 10–11, secondcorner, kuleczka, Ruth Black, MaxyM, SuriyaPhoto; 16, Moljavka; 21, Irtsya, tang; 22–23, photo_journey; 24–25, Syrytsyna Tetiana, KostanPROFF; 28–29, Nataliia Litovchenko, rizalit; 30, Nadezhda Shlemina; 33, Romanova Ekaterina; 34–39, besunnytoo; 42, AKaiser; 44, mikibith; 47, Lana L; 48, Ma-ry, Irtsya; 52, Le Panda; 56–57, vectorkat, Depiano; 60–61, photo_journey, Sundra; 62, keko-ka. Spot art on page 64 © Svetlana Bakaldina/Creative Market.

Join the community of *Ideals* readers on Facebook at: www.facebook.com/IdealsMagazine
Readers are invited to submit original poetry and prose for possible use in future publications. Please send no more than four typed submissions to: *Ideals* submissions, Worthy Publishing Group, 6100 Tower Circle, Suite 210, Franklin, Tennessee 37067. Manuscripts will be returned if a self-addressed stamped envelope is included.

ACKNOWLEDGMENTS:

GRIGSBY, MICHELLE. "An Easter Story" from www.michellegrigsby.net. Copyright © Michelle Grigsby. All rights reserved. Used by permission.

OUR THANKS to the following authors or their heirs: Georgia B. Adams, Pamela Perry Blaine, Anne Kennedy Brady, Jonathan Henderson Brooks, Esther York Burkholder, Edith Shaw Butler, Lansing Christman, Doris B. Clearman, Gertrude Dicks, Patricia B. Dye, Mabel Fundingsland, J. Harold Gwynne, Edna Jaques, Pamela Kennedy, Pamela Love, Phyllis C. Michael, Mamie Ozburn Odum, Catherine Otten, Rose Myra Phillips, Margaret L. Rorke, Edna Moore Schultz, Garnett Ann Schultz, Eileen Spinelli, Clyde L. True, Ruth H. Underhill, Beulah Sutton Waite, Diane Dean White, Roy Zylstra.

Scripture quotations, unless otherwise indicated, are taken from the King James Version (KJV). Scripture quotations marked NIV are taken from the *Holy Bible, New International Version®*, NIV® Copyright ©1973, 1978, 1984, 2011 by Biblica, Inc.® Used by permission. All rights reserved worldwide.

Every effort has been made to establish ownership and use of each selection in this book. If contacted, the publisher will be pleased to rectify any inadvertent errors or omissions in subsequent editions.